Success Tweets

For Virtual Assistants

140 Bits of Common Sense
Career Advice For Professional VAs
All in 140 Characters or Less

BUD BILANICH
The Common Sense Guy

PEGGY MURRAH

FRONT ROW PRESS

Front Row Press
191 University Boulevard, #414 • Denver, CO 80206 • 303.393.0446

This book is for our spouses, Cathy and Jeff.

xoxoxoxoxoxoxoxoxoxoxoxoxoxoxoxoxoxoxoxoxoxoxo
xoxoxoxoxoxoxoxoxoxoxoxoxoxoxoxoxoxoxoxoxoxoxo
xoxoxoxoxoxoxoxoxoxoxoxoxoxoxoxoxoxoxoxoxoxoxo
xoxoxoxoxoxoxoxoxoxoxoxoxoxoxoxoxoxoxoxoxoxoxo
xoxoxoxoxoxoxoxoxoxoxoxoxoxoxoxoxoxoxoxoxoxoxo
xoxoxoxoxoxoxoxoxoxoxoxoxoxoxoxoxoxoxoxoxoxoxo
xoxoxoxoxoxoxoxoxoxoxoxoxoxoxoxoxoxoxoxoxoxoxo

That's 140 hugs and kisses...

Introduction

This is a success book in 140 tweets. It's a real book that will help you create the professional VA success you deserve.

It gives you 140 pieces of common sense professional VA success advice, all in 140 characters or less.

It will tell you how to succeed as a professional VA, 1 tweet at a time. You'll get the essentials with no fluff.

Becoming a highly successful professional VA should be fun and exciting. This book will show you how to do it.

Your time is valuable. You don't want to waste it. That's why you get 140 pieces of advice twitter style, in 140 characters or less.

Building a successful professional VA career is simple common sense. It's not hard, but you need to do it right.

Focus on the 8 Keys to becoming a successful professional VA.

Clarify the purpose and direction for your professional VA career.

- Create clarity by figuring out what success means to you personally.
- Create clarity by creating a vivid mental image of yourself as a success.
- Create clarity by determining your personal values.

Commit to your professional VA success.

- Take personal responsibility.
- Take personal responsibility by setting and achieving high goals.

- Take personal responsibility by choosing to react positively to the people and events in your life; especially the negative ones.

Build unshakable self confidence.

- Build your confidence by choosing to be optimistic.
- Build your confidence by facing your fears and acting.
- Build your confidence by surrounding yourself with positive people.
- Build your confidence by finding a mentor to help you create your success.

Get competent.

- Get competent by becoming a lifelong learner.
- Get competent by getting fit.

- Get competent by managing your time, life and stress well.
- Get competent by learning what it takes to become a successful VA professional.

Create positive personal impact.

- Create positive personal impact by creating and nurturing your unique personal brand.
- Create positive personal impact by being impeccable in your presentation of self; in person and on line.
- Create positive personal impact by knowing and following the basic rules of business etiquette.

Become a dynamic communicator.

- Become a dynamic communicator by demonstrating strong conversation skills.

- Become a dynamic communicator by writing clearly and succinctly.
- Become a dynamic communicator by mastering public speaking skills.

Build strong relationships.

- Build relationships through self awareness. Use this knowledge to better understand others.
- Build relationships by paying it forward; give with no expectation of return.
- Build relationships by using conflict to strengthen, not weaken, relationships with the important people in your life.

Take care of yourself.

- Do what you need to feel good about yourself, your life and your professional VA career.

The tweets that follow will show you how to put these 8 Keys to work – and become the successful VA pro you deserve to be.

Will tweet books replace traditional books? Probably not. But this book will get you started as a successful VA pro.

Enjoy this book. But remember, we want to talk *with* you, not *to* you. Please tweet what you think about our ideas. @BudBilanich and @pmurrah.

Each of the points we've made above is less than 140 characters.

See? You can communicate a lot of useful information in 140 characters or less. Enjoy the following 140 tweets.

Clarity

CLARITY

1

Define exactly what becoming a successful pro VA means to you. It's easier to hit a clear, unambiguous target.

CLARITY

2

The more clear you are about what VA success means to you personally, the easier it will be to create the life you want.

SUCCESS TWEETS FOR VIRTUAL ASSISTANTS

3

Think of your purpose as your personal mission; why you are on this earth. Your direction is your vision for the next 3 to 5 years.

CLARITY

4

The mightier your purpose, the more likely you are to succeed. It will give you a strong foundation when the winds of change shift.

CLARITY

5

Your vision should be a BHAG; a Big Hairy
Audacious Goal. Make it something that
is really worth working for and
accomplishing.

CLARITY

6

Make sure you really want to be a pro VA.
Work you love will make it easier to create
the success you deserve.

CLARITY

7

Don't focus just on making money. If you do, you'll be asking too little of yourself. Focus on being useful in this world.

SUCCESS TWEETS FOR VIRTUAL ASSISTANTS

8

Happiness doesn't come from getting more things. It comes from finding a worthy purpose and pursuing it.

SUCCESS TWEETS FOR VIRTUAL ASSISTANTS

CLARITY

9

Emerson says, "Good luck is another name for tenacity of purpose." Pursue your purpose as a pro VA tenaciously.

CLARITY

10

Create a vivid mental image of your success. This vivid image will keep you motivated and moving forward when things get tough.

CLARITY

11

Think of your vivid mental image as a blueprint. It is a plan for success, but you still have to do the work to make it a reality.

CLARITY

12

Visualize the euphoria of your pro VA success, not the pain of failure.

CLARITY

13

Use affirmations to create your sales success. Affirmations are statements about the future stated in the present tense.

CLARITY

14

Clarify your personal values. They are your anchor and your guide to decision making in ambiguous situations.

CLARITY

15

Your values come from deep inside you.
Spend the time necessary to discover them.
Hold fast to them; honor them by your
actions.

Commitment

COMMITMENT

16

You're in charge! Commit to taking personal responsibility for becoming the successful pro VA you deserve to be.

COMMITMENT

17

Take personal responsibility for your success. No one will do it for you. Remember: "If it's to be, it's up to me."

COMMITMENT

18

Aim high. Set and achieve high goals –
month after month and year after year
after year. Do whatever it takes to achieve
those goals.

COMMITMENT

19

Make your goals S.M.A.R.T. : **S**pecific, **M**easurable, **A**chievable, **R**elevant and **T**ime Bound.

COMMITMENT

20

Focus on your goals several times a day. Spend your valuable time only on the things that will help you achieve them.

COMMITMENT

21

List the reasons for each goal you set for yourself. These reasons will come in handy when you get tired and frustrated.

COMMITMENT

22

Create goals in all areas of your life: career, personal, business, family, hobbies, health and fitness. Make sure they are congruent.

COMMITMENT

23

Plan how you will achieve your professional VA goals. Do whatever you have to do, not feel like doing, to achieve them.

COMMITMENT

24

Stuff will happen as you create your professional VA success. Choose to respond positively to the negative stuff.

COMMITMENT

25

Failures are the tuition you pay for success. When you have a setback, choose to react positively and learn something.

COMMITMENT

26

Persistent people keep going; especially in the face of difficulties. Keep at it; you will reach your professional VA goals.

COMMITMENT

27

Don't be afraid to fail. You fail only if you don't learn something from the experience. Treat every failure as an opportunity to grow.

COMMITMENT

28

It's not what happens to you, but how you react to it. Don't dwell on the negative, use it as a springboard to action and creativity.

COMMITMENT

29

Don't let a slow day get you down. If you come back empty handed in your quest for success, get up the next day and keep working.

COMMITMENT

30

Vision without action is a daydream. No matter how big your plans and dreams, they'll never become a reality until you act on them.

Confidence

CONFIDENCE

31

Focus on what you are becoming – a successful VA professional. This makes it easier to believe in yourself.

CONFIDENCE

32

Choose optimism. It builds your confidence. Believe that today will be better than yesterday and that tomorrow will be better yet.

CONFIDENCE

33

Optimism is contagious. Become a positive, optimistic person. Surround yourself with positive people. They will build your confidence.

CONFIDENCE

34

Everyone is afraid sometime. Self confident people face their fears and act. Look your fears in the eye and do something.

CONFIDENCE

35

Defeat fear. Here are 4 steps to deal with fears that can sabotage your success. Identify it. Admit it. Accept it. Do something about it.

CONFIDENCE

36

Procrastination is the physical manifestation of fear and is a confidence killer. Act – especially when you're afraid.

CONFIDENCE

37

Surround yourself with positive people.
Hold them close. They will give you energy
and help you create the success you want
and deserve.

CONFIDENCE

38

Jettison the negative people in your life. They are energy black holes. They will suck you dry; but only if you let them.

39

Find a mentor. Mentors are positive people who will help you find the lessons in your problems and failures and use them to move forward.

CONFIDENCE

40

Identify the self confident people you know. Pay attention to how they act and carry themselves. Watch what they do. Act like them.

CONFIDENCE

41

Fake it till you make it. Act as if you expect to be accepted, and you will be. This will boost your self confidence!

CONFIDENCE

42

Self confidence comes from within. Outside reinforcement and strokes can help, but you have to build your own confidence.

CONFIDENCE

43

Be as enthusiastic about the success of others as you are about your own. Help all the people around recognize that they are special.

CONFIDENCE

44

Give so much time to building your self confidence and improving yourself that you have no time to criticize others.

CONFIDENCE

45

Take stock of yourself. What are your strengths? What are your weaknesses? Confident people emphasize their strengths.

Competence

COMPETENCE

46

Become a lifelong learner. The half-life of knowledge is rapidly diminishing. Staying in the same place is the same as going backwards.

COMPETENCE

47

Learn as fast, or faster, than the world changes. In a world that never stops changing, you can never stop learning and growing.

COMPETENCE

48

Stay focused. Don't get distracted. Treat time as the precious commodity that it is. Manage your time and life well.

COMPETENCE

49

Break large projects into smaller chunks.
They are not so overwhelming that way.
Set mini milestones for yourself.

COMPETENCE

50

Get organized. Organize your time, life and workspace. Sweat the small stuff. Success is in execution. Execution is in the details.

COMPETENCE

51

The better you feel, the better you'll perform. Live a healthy lifestyle. Eat well. Exercise regularly. Get regular checkups.

COMPETENCE

52

Determine your peak energy times. Schedule "high brain" tasks then and "low brain" tasks at times when your energy is lowest.

COMPETENCE

53

Don't take yourself too seriously. Lighten up. It will help you master yourself and become an outstanding pro VA.

COMPETENCE

54

Get into a high performance mindset.
Don't question yourself. Trust your skills
and abilities. Do what you know how to do.

COMPETENCE

55

Good truly is the enemy of great. Don't settle for good performance. Today, good is mediocre. Become a great performer.

COMPETENCE

56

Your customer is king (or queen). Treat them like they are, and many problems will be solved before they become problems.

COMPETENCE

57

Always confirm your client's deadline. If it's unreasonable or you know you won't hit it, let your client know on the front end.

COMPETENCE

58

Check, check and re-check. Your client's business depends on your work. If she has to always double-check, you're not doing your job.

COMPETENCE

59

Being a Professional Virtual Assistant is a real job. You can't go shopping and have lunch with your friends every day. Get over it.

COMPETENCE

60

Keep a backup of all your work, whether it's a cloud account, or an external hard drive you keep somewhere else. Crashes happen.

COMPETENCE

61

Before you answer the phone, pause, take a breath and smile. You'll sound happy and calm – just what the doctor ordered for every client!

COMPETENCE

62

Make sure you understand the task at hand. It's always better to ask more questions and be clear at the start.

COMPETENCE

63

Sometimes you'll need to fire a client. While never a pleasant thing to do, if they drain your energy and passion, it's the right thing to do.

COMPETENCE

64

Don't assume your client knows what you are talking about, especially with tech topics. Break it down so a child could understand.

COMPETENCE

65

Clearly document the tasks you do. A lot happens in a month and your client may not remember everything they asked you to do.

COMPETENCE

66

Set expectations up front. It's okay to not be available evenings and weekends. Nor must you pick up the phone every time it rings.

COMPETENCE

67

Be flexible. When your client is up against a deadline, they need your support – not rigid rules.

COMPETENCE

68

Your client doesn't know what they don't know. Help them understand where they are leaving money on the table.

COMPETENCE

69

What's the next step? Your client wants to grow their business – help them. What's the next step they should take?

70

When you make a mistake (and you will), own up to it. Accept the consequences and move on.

COMPETENCE

71

If you're taking off for a few days, let your clients know. If they feel you have disappeared, they will go somewhere else.

COMPETENCE

72

Be conscientious about what you post on Twitter and Facebook. While you do have a life, you are still a Professional. Act like one.

COMPETENCE

73

Consider a daily update to your client. A post-it note on a project is like putting a smiley face on a tweet.

COMPETENCE

74

Don't promise what you know you can't deliver. Better to tell your client 'you don't know' up front than to frustrate him in the end.

COMPETENCE

75

The look and feel of your website matters. Part of your service will be to maintain your client's online presence. Make sure yours is professional.

COMPETENCE

76

Want clients? Make sure you let them know how to contact you! Have your contact information available in several places on your website.

COMPETENCE

77

Problem-solving is easier than crisis-management! Take care of even the smallest issues immediately.

COMPETENCE

78

Simple manners go a long way in the Internet world. Always be courteous and respectful, regardless of how someone else behaves toward you.

COMPETENCE

79

Think globally. Your clients will likely live outside your time zone. Note both times when you schedule calls.

COMPETENCE

80

People connect with people. Use your photo on your website and social media profiles.

COMPETENCE

81

The VA world is small. Be careful about burning bridges-there is a good chance you will cross paths with most people again.

COMPETENCE

82

Don't assume people carefully read your emails. Keep them short, to the point and outline any action items you need returned.

COMPETENCE

83

Always get to know your customer and his or her needs before you try to sell anything.

COMPETENCE

84

Build relationships constantly and continuously. Keep in touch via phone, email, text messages and the occasional handwritten note.

COMPETENCE

85

Develop TOMA with your clients – **Top Of** the **Mind Awareness**. Make sure they think of you first.

Positive Personal Impact

POSITIVE PERSONAL IMPACT

86

Create and nurture your unique personal brand. Stand, and be known for, something. Make sure that everything you do is on brand.

POSITIVE PERSONAL IMPACT

87

Your personal brand should be unique to you, but built on integrity. Integrity is doing the right thing even when no one's looking.

POSITIVE PERSONAL IMPACT

88

Build your personal brand. Do whatever it takes to make sure that people will think of and remember you in the way you want them to.

POSITIVE PERSONAL IMPACT

89

Nurture your network. What your friends, colleagues, clients, and customers say about you is how others will think of your brand.

POSITIVE PERSONAL IMPACT

90

Demonstrate respect for yourself and others in your dress. People will notice and respond positively to you.

POSITIVE PERSONAL IMPACT

91

Be well groomed and appropriate for every situation. Always dress one level up from what is expected. You'll stand out from the crowd.

92

"Business" is the first and most important word in "business casual". Dress like you're going to work, not a sporting event or club.

93

21st Century technology has created new etiquette rules. Learn and use them to appear polished when you're on line.

POSITIVE PERSONAL IMPACT

94

Be gracious. Know and follow the basic rules of etiquette. Everybody likes to be around polite and mannerly people.

POSITIVE PERSONAL IMPACT

95

When someone compliments you, just say "thank you". When someone criticizes you, say "thank you, I'll work on that".

POSITIVE PERSONAL IMPACT

96

Learn and use simple table manners.
Good manners make you look polished
and poised and help you concentrate on
the conversation.

POSITIVE PERSONAL IMPACT

97

Always act like a lady or gentleman. It's not old fashioned; it's smart business and leads to a successful life and career.

POSITIVE PERSONAL IMPACT

98

Keep your breath fresh. Brush after meals
and coffee. Use the strips. Don't chew
gum. Ever. It makes you look like a cow.

POSITIVE PERSONAL IMPACT

99

Say "thank you" often. You'll succeed in your life and career, build a strong personal brand and leave a legacy of being a nice person.

POSITIVE PERSONAL IMPACT

100

Be courteous. It costs you nothing, and it can mean everything to someone else. It also helps in getting what you want.

Dynamic Communication

DYNAMIC COMMUNICATION

101

All dynamic communicators have mastered three basic communication skills: conversation, writing and presenting.

DYNAMIC COMMUNICATION

102

Speak from your heart. Show that you care – about yourself and the people with whom you are speaking.

DYNAMIC COMMUNICATION

103

A brief conversation with the right person can greatly help – or hinder your success as a pro VA.

DYNAMIC COMMUNICATION

104

Conversation tips: be warm, pleasant, gracious and sensitive to the interpersonal needs and anxieties of others.

DYNAMIC COMMUNICATION

105

Demonstrate your understanding of others' points of view. Listen well and ask questions if you don't understand.

DYNAMIC COMMUNICATION

106

Become an excellent conversationalist by listening more than speaking. Pay attention to what other people say; respond appropriately.

DYNAMIC COMMUNICATION

107

Live people take precedence over phone calls. So continue in person, face to face conversations, rather than answering your cell phone.

DYNAMIC COMMUNICATION

108

Use the 2/3 – 1/3 rule. Listen two thirds of the time; speak one third of the time. Focus your complete attention on the other person.

DYNAMIC COMMUNICATION

109

Remember and use people's names. Look for common ground with the people you meet. Find out about them, their hobbies and passions.

DYNAMIC COMMUNICATION

110

Become a clear, concise writer. Make your writing easy to read and easy to understand. Use simple straightforward language.

111

Write clearly and simply: short words and sentences; first person; active voice. Be precise in your choice of words.

DYNAMIC COMMUNICATION

112

Become an excellent presenter. Script
your talk. Practice until you are perfect.

DYNAMIC COMMUNICATION

113

Presentation steps: 1) Determine the message. 2) Analyze the audience. 3) Organize the information. 4) Design visuals. 5) Practice.

114

Presentations are easy to create. Write your closing first, your opening next. Then fill in the content. Practice, practice, practice.

DYNAMIC COMMUNICATION

115

Discipline yourself to prepare for presentations. Practice out loud until you are totally in sync with what you're going to say.

Relationship Building

RELATIONSHIP BUILDING

116

Get genuinely interested in others. Help bring out the best in everyone you know. Others will gravitate to you.

RELATIONSHIP BUILDING

117

Use every social interaction to build
and strengthen relationships. Strong
relationships are your ticket to success
as a pro VA.

118

Everyone has something to offer. Never dismiss anyone out of hand. Take the initiative. Actively build relationships with others.

119

Get to know yourself. Use your self knowledge to better understand others and build mutually beneficial relationships with them.

RELATIONSHIP BUILDING

120

Pay it forward. Build strong relationships by giving of yourself and your time with no expectation of return.

RELATIONSHIP BUILDING

121

When meeting someone new ask yourself, "What can I do to help this person?" By thinking this first, you'll build stronger relationships.

RELATIONSHIP BUILDING

122

There is no quid pro quo in effective relationships. Do for others without being asked or waiting for them to do for you.

RELATIONSHIP BUILDING

123

Be generous. By giving with no expectation of return, you'll be surprised by how much comes back to you in the long run.

RELATIONSHIP BUILDING

124

Be happy to see others succeed. Use the success of others to motivate yourself to greater success.

RELATIONSHIP BUILDING

125

Trust is the glue that holds relationships together. The more you demonstrate trust in others, the more they will trust you.

RELATIONSHIP BUILDING

126

Resolve conflict positively. Treat conflict as an opportunity to strengthen, not destroy, the relationships you've worked hard to build.

127

Be a consensus builder. Focus on where you agree with other people. It will be easier to resolve differences and create agreement.

RELATIONSHIP BUILDING

128

Be responsible for yourself. No one can "make you angry". Choose to act in a civil, forthright, constructive manner in tense situations.

RELATIONSHIP BUILDING

129

We all make mistakes. Own up to yours. You'll become known as a straight shooter – honest with yourself and with others.

RELATIONSHIP BUILDING

130

Become widely trusted. Deliver on what you say you'll do. If you can't meet a commitment, let the other person know right away.

Take Care
Of Yourself

131

Be kind to yourself. Accept yourself. Love yourself and who you are.

TAKE CARE OF YOURSELF

132

Take care of yourself. Do what you need to do to feel good about yourself, your life and your professional VA career.

TAKE CARE OF YOURSELF

133

Choose to be you – don't wait for other people's permission to live your life and pursue your professional VA success.

TAKE CARE OF YOURSELF

134

Be hopeful and abundant. Hope defeats fear. Abundance defeats scarcity.

TAKE CARE OF YOURSELF

135

You get what you expect. Expect the best as a pro VA and you'll get it.

TAKE CARE OF YOURSELF

136

When you focus on what's going right in your life, things will begin going right more often.

TAKE CARE OF YOURSELF

137

Blame, resentments and envy get in the way of taking care of yourself and creating the sales success you deserve.

138

Forgiveness precedes peace and harmony. Forgive others. More important, forgive yourself.

TAKE CARE OF YOURSELF

139

Every morning when you wake up, envision yourself as having a great day, filled with success and happiness.

TAKE CARE OF YOURSELF

140

Every night before you go to sleep, think about the good things that happened to you that day. Sleep in appreciation of them.

ONE MORE THING

141

And, because we always over deliver, here is one more very important tweet…

Knowing is not enough. Successful pro VAs will act on this advice. Take action. Become the successful pro VA we know you can be.

About The Authors

@BudBilanich, a life and career success coach helping you create the success you deserve. Let me help you succeed: www.BudBilanich.com.

@pmurrah, Online Business Manager. Owner of PMA Web Services, a full service VA firm. Geek. Mom of three boys. More at PeggyMurrah.com.

Success Tweets for Virtual Assistants
makes a great gift!

Quantity discounts are available
from the publisher.

Call 303.393.0446 to inquire
about quantity pricing.